Anunnaki Return, Star Nations and the Days to Come

Star Nation Manual, the Hidden Knowledge and Path to Planetary Healing and Self-Empowerment.

Bringing awareness to the Andromedans, Arcturians, Orion Council of Light, Pleiadians and Sirian Star Nations involved in the Awakening and Healing of Humanity and the Earth.

By James Gilliland

ISBN 978-1-329-92564-9

Chapters

Credits

Thanks to the ECETI family and all of its supporters

Susan McAliley (Cover Photo and Art Work)

Steve and Evan Strong
www.forgottonorigin.com

Peter Maxwell Slattery
www.petermaxwellslattery.com
www.ecetiaustralia.com

Solreta Antaria
www.solretapsychicreadings.com
www.ecetiaustralia.com

Uluki Brendan Murray (Elder and King of the Raven Tribe)

Alan (Aboriginal Elder) and Pancake (Local)

And the beautiful and hospitable people of OZ (Australia)

Chapter 1
The Anunnaki and Misperceptions

There are a lot of stories about the Anunnaki, the beings who came from Heaven to Earth in ancient times. They came for gold to repair their atmosphere and found an Earth human, what you would call Neanderthal and added their genes to the mix to create a better, stronger, wiser human. It was not a slave race. The hybrid they created was in awe of their creators and willingly served them. It was a win, win situation, a quantum leap in evolution, a wiser more powerful body, increasing access to the higher dimensions and an incarnation far beyond what was available to them at the time. This was a trade in genetics for service to help them preserve and restore their planet. These wise and powerful beings knew about karma, they knew about universal law and were very careful not to step outside universal law in their actions. They knew they were crossing the line and their rules forbid interference in primitive cultures yet they chose to overlook this due to the need for self-preservation of their colony on Nibiru. After they left Earth there were several settlements where the Anunnaki left in charge a group of their own to oversee the evolution of their creations. This relationship was not as master and servant in the beginning, it was as elder brothers and sisters to guide these beginning civilizations. The ones they left behind were revered as the Gods. Unfortunately those they left behind fell in consciousness over time, bred with their creations, created demigods and got lost in the power struggles and more primitive emotions over time. These magnificent beings were known as the bearded Gods, this is where most of humanity got their image of God. They are often depicted as working side by side with the Feline or Lion beings, the benevolent

7

protectors. They were not reptilian they are your ancestors genetically tied to Earth very spiritually and technologically advanced beings.

The Anunnaki are returning. This has many on Earth scrambling because they are out of alignment with universal law as clearly demonstrated by the condition of this civilization and the environment. They will be seen as a threat, portrayed as merciless Gods and conquerors we all must fear yet this is all perpetuated by the controllers on Earth. Those operating outside of universal law who have misled, manipulated and enslaved humanity for thousands of years. Those seen and unseen forces; which find their presence, their wisdom, love and extremely advanced spiritual technologies a threat.

The Anunnaki are not coming to conquer you they are coming to free you. I have been in contact with one known as Enha. She is a Goddess and her love and healing abilities are beyond measure. She is a welcome breath of fresh air in these times and it will take beings such as these to turn this civilization and planet around. Very few can stand before these beings. Their frequencies are too high for most and it is no wonder those of a baser nature, those in fear, guilt, feeling unworthy or those who choose greed, power over others cannot be in their presence or might feel them as a threat. It is like Mama and Daddy are coming home and the kids have severely misbehaved and forgotten their roots. Yet like most loving parents all their kids have to do is stop misbehaving. We can turn to these beings for healing, guidance along with the beautiful many other saints, sages, masters, and spiritually and technologically advanced off-worlder and ultradimensionals. Those dedicated to empowering the individual to make their own personal God/Creator/Spirit connection. We are going to need all the help we can get to clean up the seen and unseen regenerate beings that have gone astray on Earth.

Enha, Golden Goddess 9th dimensional being with Anunnaki Council of 12

Kael past life as Demigod, half human half Anunnaki

Chapter 2
The Gods, Demigods, and Ascended Masters.

There are 6th through 9th dimensional beings that would appear to humanity as Gods. There are those who maintain an appearance best known to humanity but in truth they are pure light beings. Just as Enha appeared to me as a Golden Goddess from Egyptian times, Cazekiel can appear as both male or female due to the fact that Casia, a female merged with Ezekiel of old and ascended. To me Cazekiel took on the form of a golden God being. His long hair flowed into his beard, which flowed into golden robes yet it consisted of magnetized light. The books Reunion With Source and Becoming Gods were the inspiration of Cazekiel. Cazekiel is known throughout the Omniverse as the 7th dimensional God of Eternal Bliss. The benevolent Anunnaki are in the 6th through 9th dimensions, the fallen ones are stuck in the 4th due to beliefs and actions outside of Universal Law.

Cazekiel God of Eternal Bliss Appearing in ECETI Field of Dreams. Photo by Kan

The Ascended Masters are in the 5th through 7th. Mother Mary has appeared to me since 5 years old. I was dying in the hospital from Bronchial Pneumonia and she appeared to me on several occasions helping me to get through the night. She has also appeared at my bedside when nefarious entities of ill intent appeared instructing me to face them without fear. Mary is a universal being not owned by any one religion. In fact she is extremely unhappy with where the Catholic Church has gone. Here message at Fatima expressed that in no uncertain terms. That is why it has been suppressed. Mary Magdalene was never a whore; she was of Royal heritage an adept trained in the Egyptian Mystery Schools. In fact it has been recently discovered that Jesus, Or Joshua bin Joseph his real name in his own words said out of all of his disciples Mary is the most qualified to carry on with his teachings. The House of Mary has always been the group Jesus most aligned with. It was a very large gathering and is coming back together in the days to come. There is a massive infusion of the Divine Feminine to bring balance back to the Earth. Jesus said on these two laws lie all the laws and the prophets. Love God with all your heart and your neighbor as yourself. It was the law of Love. Muktananda once said there are two reasons for every action, Love and the lack of love. The house of Mary is the house of Love. It is aligned with the Shakina Energies, The divine feminine and has many levels. It seems many of the known Ascended Masters (Male and Female), can appear in the 5th through the 7th. Some can even manifest in a physical body yet it consists of a denser form of magnetized light. The Ascended Masters like us are also interdimensional. We can have a Master appear to us on the 4th, 5th, 6th on up to the 9th in their own higher vibrational body. After the NDE, near death experience I did not want to talk with anyone but Jesus due to prior programming. All the rest were spooks and I did not have the training or the teachers to help me understand the experience.

Mother Mary Appearing at ECETI Self Mastery Class.
Photo By Kan

After many appearances and teachings on an inner level Jesus appeared with Baba Ji. Baba Ji is known as the Yogi Christ I then was instructed to learn the Eastern disciplines resulting in 11 years of Yoga along with initiations from various Yogis. When that was completed Jesus again came with White Eagle a Native American Master Teacher. Again I was instructed to learn the Native American ways resulting in many ceremonies and working with many Elders. I was also instructed and initiated by Lamas from Tibet. Then began the Ultradimensional Teachings from the Pleiadians, Orion Council of Light, Andromedans, Sirians, and Last the Arcturians. The very latest contacts have been with the benevolent Anunnaki, one particular was Enha a 9th dimensional being on the Council of Twelve. These are the original Anunnaki, which never fell and still operate under Universal Law. I was then told they were here to right a wrong, a grand recall of the fallen ones is occurring. The ones who strayed from Universal law in the 3rd and 4th dimensions are being forced to stand in front of the Council of Twelve and explain their actions. This is not without consequences. The benevolent Anunnaki are also involved in cleaning up the Archonic or Draconian system that infiltrated the Earth over 400,000 years ago due to an invitation by Marduk.

Reptilians along with fallen Anunnaki. Marduk's unholy alliance.

There are major families, which call themselves the Sons of Marduk, the Bush's and Banksters, which might shed a little light on why the Earth is in its present predicament. They are the war and disease profiteers.

There were great wars, meteor impacts, pole shifts all of which created a reset on the Earth. During these great wars and shifts the Anunnaki had to move due to the extreme nature of the weapons used, some of which were atomic in nature. The Greek Gods were the Anunnaki. That is where we acquired the image of the Bearded God. They had children with Earth humans called demigods. Noah, Samson, Hercules etc. were all demigods. The major religions reflected the behavior and beliefs of different Anunnaki rulers. To be religious and worship an external God is not enlightened. To be brutally honest it is barbaric and ignorant living in the past. I know to some this will sound very blasphemous yet every enlightened master referred to the temple as within. Know your true history. It is the belief in external Gods and saviors straying from Universal Law along with avoiding personal responsibility that has created this mess. Finding God within an internal process is the way out. Religions separate, they each have their images of God and their prophets yet who created them? Unity Consciousness does not separate and the grand shift is the alignment with Unity Consciousness. Transcending all cultural and religious beliefs that separate is the path. We all came from the same source and we all return to the same source thus we are all connected as one big family. Omnipresence means everywhere present. The Creator is omnipresent within all Creation the source of all Creation. It is the unified field. The Star Nations have come and gone reminding us of this while reseeding the Earth allowing new civilizations to spring forward. This is the 5th world and we are all hoping it does not follow the same path as the previous worlds. This is up to us.

Baba Ji appearing at ECETI Photo by Kan

Chapter 3

The Andromedans

When we speak of the Andromedans again we have to realize it is a very big galaxy. There are many different races living within and coming from that galaxy. There is the Andromedan Council which is one of the highest Councils upon which the Pleiadians, Orion Council of Light, the benevolent Star Nations go to for inspiration and guidance. Some of the Andromedans are mythologically known as ArchAngels. They have magnetized light bodies seen as eight to ten feet tall and exist in a holographic light universe. They have their magnificent light ships, which would blot out your entire northern sky. When discovered by the Pleiadians they were in awe. They asked them to guide them, council them, be their leaders. The Andromedans refused telling them you need to lead yourselves. They did however agree to inspire and guide yet the decisions would always be left up to the Pleiadians as to their self-determination. It is not uncommon to see guiding councils with an Andromedan involved, there are some that are very tall and blue skinned as well. Believe it or not, some have incarnated on Earth. Others have materialized a body to interact with people on Earth assisting in the awakening and healing process. It is as if God has given its best for these times to assist humanity make the transition. God's best are also humans awakening to their divine heritage. The Andromedans are now taking an active part in the restoration of Earth. They are great for protection and transcending to the highest levels of consciousness.

Chapter 4

Pleiadian Assistance

We first must know the true history of the Earth before we go into the nature of the Pleiadians. Your Earth has had advanced races of beings setting up colonies for over 600 million years. Your most ancient colonies are beneath oceans or ice, some have been recycled as the plates move the Earth expands and are now molten rock or beneath the oceans due to pole and crustal shifts. Some are buried under sand; earth and jungles have covered others. The forbidden sciences or oops art archeological findings which do not fit into the mainstream story are testimony of this. The evidence has been destroyed or stored with the Smithsonian and under the Vatican never to see the light of day because they are in direct opposition with the stories told by major religions and science. There are ancient stories passed down with many indigenous cultures of the Star Nations, ancient astronauts, the flying vehicles of the gods and great battles in the heavens and on Earth. These are not legends they are facts about real time events in ancient history. The ancient Vedic texts are replete with these stories even the Bible for those with open minds and critical thinking.

The Pleiadians fit into these ancient legends. They were the Terra formers of ancient times along with other Star Nations and have more genetic stock on Earth than any other race. Because of this they were passed the scepter according to universal law to assist humanity and the Earth in the great transition yet they are not alone. There were 12 Star Nations who were the main players in the Terra forming of Earth. They came after the Anunnaki around 18,000 years ago. There is a place known as the

Gosford Glyphs where this is all written in stone. There are ancient Egyptian glyphs carved in stone on one side, Pleiadian glyphs on the other. The Pleiadian glyphs tell a story of the beginning of man, how a primitive man already existing here was tampered with genetically creating the original people. The Aboriginals are the original people and their genetics are found throughout the world. The Egyptian glyphs tell of two Pharaohs who came to Australia to steal the original knowledge. The Elders told them they could not take the knowledge with them, which was most likely written on stones. One was bitten by a poisonous snake and died. He was buried at the Gosford Glyphs. The other died in a shipwreck. There is the Australian Stone Henge, which dates much older than the one in England. England and the Azores are the mountaintops where the survivors of the great flood started over. The latest research by Steve and Evan Strong has proven the Pleiadian connection and the fact that humanity actually had its origins in Australia. www.forgottenorigin.com

James with Steve & Evan Strong

I would strongly advise not to go to these sacred sites without an Elder or without contacting the Strongs. There is a special way of entering the glyphs, a ceremony has to be done properly asking permission. There are also proper ways and paths to take. Women need to be accompanied by men and they must stay together. There are places for the women where men cannot go and places for the men where women cannot go. To act disrespectful can have serious consequences in illness, accidents and death.

Gosford Glyphs clearly Egyptian

More Egyptian Glyphs

Guardian at opening to Glyphs. It is said if they are not present pack up and go home.

Laying down in Star Gate to make contact.

Pleiadian Craft on Pleiadian glyph wall

Chapter 5
Uluki Brendan Murray

One of the Elders I met on my trip to Australia was Uluki Brendan Murray. He is the King of the Raven Tribe in the Yarra Valley and represents three other tribes. He is prophesized to be the one to bring out the hidden knowledge when it is time. We spent a long time sharing stories and knowledge about the ancient times. His stories matched with my earlier research along with the Native American stories on Turtle Island, "America". Just as most indigenous Elders point to the Pleiades as their origins so do the Aboriginals. He shared with us the origins of Uluru, Kata Tjuta, which originated from the Pleiades and other ancient knowledge. Just as it began in Australia it will end in Australia. You will have to read between the lines because I cannot reveal at this time the rest of the story. As a little hint it has everything to do with the Anunnaki Return.

On the way to meet with Brendan odd anomalies occurred with ravens. Previously with Peter Slattery our ECETI Australia representative ravens kept appearing all along the way. When we went together the same anomalies happened only this time two eagles kept appearing with them. This continued throughout our journey. The most incredible event happened when we went to Westall where the ships came over the local school and landed. This is a very famous UFO case file. They actually built a playground with a UFO, swings, slides other playground equipment along with signs documenting the event. Unlike America who hides these events the Australian government actually made a monument to the event. When we stepped into the park where the UFO landed we could see the trees all bent inward. There was another area where one touched down and the grass is still bare. While we were doing a documentary the ravens began to come. Hundreds and hundreds of ravens. The trees were full and they were circling us cawing while group after group appeared. It was like a scene out of Alfred Hitchcock, "The Birds". This time it was an initiation into the Raven Tribe. It was hilarious, so over the top no one could not agree in the phenomena. Locals said they have never seen this before.

Upon returning home Brendan told us it was an initiation, welcome to the family. I would keep an eye on Australia and the aboriginal movement. Big changes will come out of this that will affect the global scene. They are the keepers of the sacred ancient knowledge, the original people. They are not only aware of the ancient origins of man, they never lost contact with the Star Nations just as many Native American Nations. There is a grand reunion in the wind and only those who can talk to the wind will know the time, location, and the outcome.

James with Uluki Brendan Murray

Ravens at Westall

The Pleiadians are fulfilling a prophecy known to most indigenous people and that prophecy is exponentially unfolding. There are many prophecies about the splitting of societies, those who will seek Creator and want to live in harmony with humanity and the Earth and those who will seek a separative path of self service, greed, division and power over others. This split in consciousness was the demise of Atlantis and Lemuria or Mu. The Pleiadians are here to assist those who seek the first path, assisting in restoring universal law and Gaia in her birthing process into a new age. Those who choose the path of separation, againstness, greed and disharmony, the path of tyranny are on a downward spiral; which will not be frequency specific to the new Earth. This process is a natural cycle, a process no man can stop and the energies and forces behind this cycle are beyond imagination.

It is as if God is invading Earth right down to the atom itself. When we speak of God it is a frequency and a force guided by divine intelligence not the images of man. It moves through the entire electromagnetic spectrum and dimensions higher than our 3d reality on Earth to and through the Earth. The Earth and this entire solar system are moving into a new highly energized place in space. There is an alignment with Galactic Plane, the center of the Milky Way galaxy, Sirius, and Alcyon; which will expose this solar system to consciousness, light and magnetic waves never before experienced by this civilization. This present civilization is the remnants of past civilizations some of which did experience these major earth changes and shifts. Stories of these great shifts have been passed down by word of mouth or written in stone such as the Mayan Calendar, pyramids and other ancient sacred sites yet very few have fully understood the information. The return of the Star

Nations and their assistance in these times is one such story yet this assistance has been greatly misunderstood through the wants and desires of those passing on their messages.

The Star Nations are here to inspire, support and assist most, of which are in unseen ways. They are assisting those who have the intention to heal and live according to universal law. They are working through the consciousness and energy grids on the planet. All thought and belief has a frequency. Base thoughts of fear, anger, jealousy, envy, religious separation and the need to control or dominate all have a lower frequency. Thoughts of love, joy, bliss, and service to others seeing the Creator in All Creation, unity consciousness are of a higher frequency. Your vibration is established by the myriad of thoughts one holds as their beliefs. The old wounds, traumas, grudges, fears and unfinished business of the past are coming to the surface to be healed. This is within the physical, mental, and emotional bodies of humanity as well as the Earth. This process also includes other planes and dimensions unaware to most. When you increase the consciousness and energy down through the vibrational continuum to a planet of a baser nature the baser lower frequency attitudes and emotions must rise to the occasion and match the new frequencies. When this happens individual and collective consciousness goes through a major transition. Social, economic and even physical Earth changes follow the influxes of energy. We will go deeper into the source and nature of these energies at a later date. Just realize this planet and all its inhabitants are going on a journey in which no one can hide or stop. The main purpose of the Pleiadians is to release the past assisting us in our awakening and healing process. Our past is creating our

31

tomorrow. Many old wounds, traumas, wrong conclusions from past experiences, old unforgiven grudges both individually and collectively are creating your tomorrow. These old patterns are even psychometrized into the land. This is in the process of being lifted and healed via spiritual technologies and telepathic interaction.

Chapter 6
Misunderstandings about Pleiadian Consciousness

We spoke about the Terra Formers yet few understand those who participate in this endeavor on the highest level. A Pleiadian, or any other spiritually advanced being when coming upon a great forest knows the consciousness and energy dynamics of that forest. They see the great tree, anchored within it the main diva or spirit of the forest. They feel the connection with that diva and the divas' connection with the entire forest. They are also aware of the energy dynamics and the templates in the etheric realm with plant and animal life. They do not just come on metal ships with high technology. Their ships are alive. Some of their ships are floating eco systems with forests, jungles, lakes, animals, etc. perfectly balanced. These are the great mother ships. Even their clothing is alive vibrating with energy. Because of their high vibration, the light emanating from their being causes flowers to bloom and birds sing in their presence even at night. They understand unity consciousness, the interconnection and source of all life, how to live in harmony with all life. This is their greatest gift and if applied will bring heaven on Earth. They walk as enlightened beings with the gifts of enlightenment. They are telepathic, can bi-locate, levitate, inspire and heal. Their technology is a reflection of their consciousness.

They are extremely spiritually and technologically advanced. Most of humanity cannot comprehend their culture unless they have taken the time to awaken the God/Creator/Spirit within. Great Yogis, Lamas, Masters,

Saints and Sages who have transcended the cultural and religious boundaries into seeing the Creator in all Creation have the best understanding; which is why these ships are often seen over temples, ashrams and sacred sites. They are inspiring and healing those who have chosen to awaken, heal and live a life in harmony with each other and Nature. They are not here to go to war with the dark hearts, the disconnected who lust for power and wealth at the expense of humanity and nature. They are here to inspire and heal, to reset Earth back on its original intent. Unfortunately their very presence is a threat to the dark hearts; which have hijacked the Earth and thrive on the pain and suffering promoting fear and separation. This is coming to a close and the Pleiadians as well as the other Star Nations play an integral part in this process. They are fulfilling the Star Nation Prophesies.

Blaji 340 year old Pleiadian Master Teacher coming
back from 2 million years in our future.

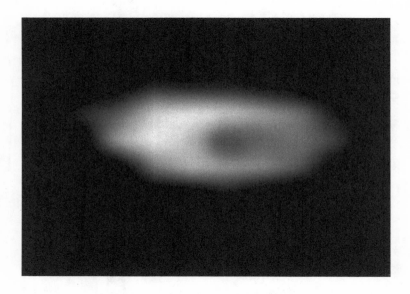

Blaji's ship which flew over ECETI during 2010
Conference Intention Experiment.

Chapter 7

The Orion Council of Light

There is much disinformation about the Orion system and it is time to shed some light on this matter. There were great wars fought throughout this system and others with the regenerate ETs against the descendants of Lyra. There were many other races involved in these wars. The regenerate ETs in the beginning caught many spiritually and technologically advanced people off guard. War and aggression was not part of their consciousness nor was it acknowledged as a threat. These peaceful people could not understand how anyone could be so ignorant as to universal law and the unified field. They also believed if they were not a threat and had no weapons war would not come to them. Unfortunately this truth was not the way of the regenerates, those who lived by war and aggression; which conquered and pillaged everywhere they went. It was a very hard lesson.

The Orion Council of Light is operating on the fifth and sixth dimension with other allies on the 3rd through 7th. They took the lesson they learned all the way to the 5th and sixth dimension which is to acknowledge the negative, find balance and always maintain one's self authority even if it means the use of force in areas where universal law is broken, an imbalance occurs or the regenerates threaten the evolution of a civilization. This is the case on Earth as we speak yet it is soon to be corrected. These beings are very strong in character, they are the great initiators and many have incarnated on Earth for these times. They are being activated through a process where when the time is right and the initiate sincerely asks a very intense process ensues.

My own personal initiation was in a bathtub during a meditation. I was tired of all the ships buzzing around on high and told the universe I want to know what this has to do with me, what is my connection and part in this. I also made it clear I wanted to know no matter what the cost. Shortly after I was hit in the chest with a beam of golden light. Three golden balls of energy came down the beam and each one was a download of consciousness, my ancient memories were returned some of which involved lives on Earth as well as off world lives. It was like watching a movie of a lifetime that only lasted a few seconds yet the full emotional experience of that life was transferred. I was teleported out of body to the ship where a short conversation with a feminine being who went by the name of Melia. This encounter was followed by a warning that I could not stay. If I stayed too long I could not function on Earth. My frequencies would be changed to a level where I could no longer adjust to society. She has maintained telepathic contact to this day.

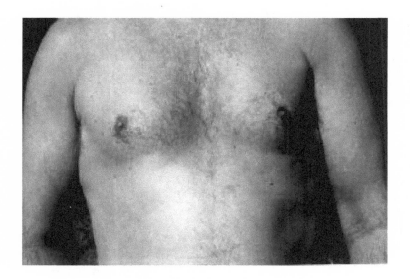

Burn Mark left by golden beam, which hit James chest, totally painless, no negative impact. Burn morphed from circle to heart shape then a triangle.

Melia from the Orion Council of Light.

My second encounter was with a being by the name of Haog. His mission was to monitor and correct the energy dispensations on Earth. If the awakening and healing energies became too intense war could break out. If the energies were too weak evolution would cease. Keeping balance in the vibrational lifting or the awakening and healing process was of the utmost importance. His ship was in charge of this process as well as monitoring any regenerate ET activity and if necessary to nullify it. This process has to be done within universal law. It is imperative not to interfere in the evolutionary process or take away lessons necessary for soul evolution. Many challenges on Earth are necessary for soul evolution and in some cases what may be seen as negative ends up being empowering if one rises to the occasion. In circumstances where the Earth may be harmed beyond her ability to repair or too many innocents are harmed by regenerates or their puppets intervention is necessary. Yet while the masses turn a blind eye and are willing participants of injustices there are times where a collective lesson or karmic backlash may be necessary.

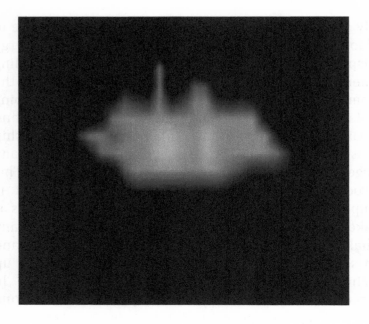

Orion Cruiser as big as an aircraft carrier.
Photo by Steve Mareno

Chapter 8

Why most of the UFO Community and Governments have not made contact with the Benevolents

Most of the contacts are being made with those who have open minds, loving hearts and pure intent. Those who truly wish to serve humanity and the Earth without hidden agendas or an unhealed past are the ones most suitable for contact. One does not have to be perfect, or a rocket scientist, healing and awakening will come along the way. One's heart must be open and directed in the proper manner. The intellect is a drop in the sea of consciousness; your emotional body operates far beyond the ability of the intellect with more resources to draw upon. Being locked in the intellect and closed down emotionally or spiritually will block any contact with higher intelligence. Most of what people are taught in the main stream curriculum is recycled ignorance. One has to step outside the intellectual box to truly understand the multidimensionality of contact yet few can let go of their beliefs, due to vested interests and fear of stepping out of the herd.

Unfortunately many who reveal themselves as experts in the field of ufology due to degrees and education in a system that denies off world visitors have the pulpit in mainstream and alternative media. They have not experienced a craft and do not know about the occupants, their culture or agenda yet have no problem taking on the handle of expert. This is not rational thinking and should be seen as such. There are those who have insider information from governments yet governments have not met the protocols necessary for contact with spiritually and technologically advanced off-worlders. Most in the world of officialdom do not have a clue concerning off world visitors especially when it comes to the ultradimensionals or the spiritually and technologically advanced civilizations. Yet people cling to authority figures to tell them the truth. When governments and institutions have a long history of lies and deceptions it is a form of insanity to expect them to do anything other than lie, deceive or twist the truth to meet their agendas. If the people actually knew how many were paid disinformants, controlled opposition only there to steer or gather information in the field of ufology holding positions in the highest ranks they would be shocked. There are those who are acting on this disinformation unknowingly, those with over active imaginations, those who are still seeking acceptance and approval outside themselves with a major monetary and ego investment. They are delivering the disempowering, feel good messages, no worries you will all be beamed up, we will clean up the mess etc. This is in direct conflict with universal law. There are those who are creating dark fearful messages due to their own victim patterns and even religious zealots trying to paint their own pictures of off-worlders in black and white. Very few call them angels, most refer to them as demons. Ufology has turned into a convoluted mess of denial, disinformation, misinformation, and people's own anthropomorphized projections as to the nature of the ships, their occupants, and higher dimensional beings. Many having no reference points, all of which have been understood from the mind that perceives them.

Pure energy ship over Mt Adams.

There is a saying, "The mind in which you seek, is the mind in which you connect." Those of higher mind will connect and contact higher minded beings yet do not believe you will not be challenged in this endeavor. There are those of a lower mind and ill intent seen and unseen that will rear their ugly heads to stop this process. Those who seek power and wealth at the expense of humanity and the Earth, those who want to control, enslave and dominate others, those who seek notoriety and financial gain as first priority, and those in the unseen who also have ill intent who care nothing for humanity and the Earth. Some - even despising both - will do all they can to keep you ignorant, distracted and disempowered. All the above is present in the field of ufology.

Very few have met the protocols for contact with spiritually and technologically advanced beings thus very few in the UFO community are having contact and are receiving accurate information that serves humanity and the Earth. The majority of contacts are outside of government and religious institutions. They are outside of mainstream media and are far and few between. The contacts are with those who align with Unity Consciousness, see the Creator in all Creation, those who have transcended all cultural and religious boundaries aligned with service to others. The enlightened ones are the ones having contact, those with a high degree of integrity; those who love and serve are the one most likely to have contact. Women far outweigh the men in this arena due to their emotional body in most cases being developed beyond the emotional body of men.

Many are being contacted, not even knowing the source of the contact, yet are still being guided on humanities' behalf. They will project their images and names on the contact often due to religious beliefs or previously accepted programs. One of the problems with telepathic contact or channeling is it is only as clear as the mind it comes through. It has to come through the mind here on Earth where the messages are often distorted by the mental, emotional and astral bodies. The more clear the mind and subtle bodies the clearer the message. It is imperative to meditate, do process oriented healing to clear wounds, traumas, wrong conclusions from past experiences to bring through a clear message. One has to get off the victim, savior, persecutor triangle; the ever-spinning wheel through deep meditation best done in nature. It takes a dedicated life to spirit, service to humanity and the Earth and loving detachment to avoid

46

all the entanglements of Earth. This is necessary to hold the consciousness to maintain contact with benevolent, spiritually and technologically advanced off-worlders and ultradimensionals. Very few can afford the lifestyle of simplicity to keep a calm mind and not be distracted by the social consciousness and demands of Earth society.

"Contact is not an external awareness, it is an internal awareness. It is not waiting for some external authority to tell you it is okay, it is developing an internal authority. Contact comes with enlightenment."

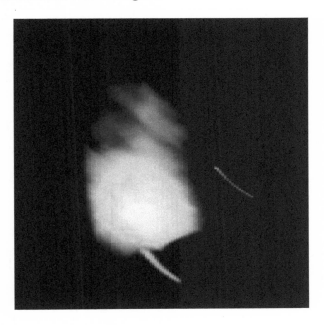

James on stage at IUFOC conference turning into a blue and green light. Ten foot tall beings were also photographed standing behind James.

Chapter 9
The Incorruptibles

There is a group of souls who are coming forward in every arena known as the incorruptibles. They operate with a direct hook up to their subconscious mind and are guided by soul and spirit. They are very aware and adept at Universal Law in full knowledge of the consequences of operating outside of it. Their words are like swords and few can be in their presence for any extended time. They resonate on a very high vibration and sometimes just their thoughts alone will bring awareness to situations that need healing or clarity. They are grand mirrors of everything people love and hate about themselves, which can be a very hard path with few true friends. Everyone wants to know them, they are champions of truth yet few people can walk with them.

The powers that were, find them very annoying because they see through the manipulations, double speak, lies and deceptions. The ones who hate them the most are the ones who have lied to and deceived the most, including themselves. They definitely do not fit into the network or mainstream and are a constant reminder of the ills of society. They know themselves; they know of the divine potential in others and are often met with jealousy or judgment by those who are not expressing their divine potential. They often teach by asking questions, usually have a wicked sense of humor and use that humor to make their points known. They are unlimited in their expression and without judgment can express any way they choose on any level. They are not bound by schisms and have transcended all religious and cultural boundaries. In others words, they are often, "PC incorrect."

You will often find them laughing and blissed out for no reason. They are often heard having conversations with unseen entities or themselves. Mainstream will have all kinds of labels for them, mainly due to being outside their control. They will always be authentic; you won't see them in sandals and white robes unless coming out of the bath or shower. In most cases you will never recognize them because they live a simple life and don't want to be recognized. They are often sovereign in nature and have mastered loving detachment. If they take a partner it is usually due to a deep soul connection not a mainstream program or false desire of the ego. The Earth is in dire need of these incorruptible souls. Although you may meet one it is much better to become one.

Chapter 10
Multidimensional Awareness

We are going to tell you a story about Pleiadian consciousness which is not unlike your own yet they reside in a more expanded awareness of the unified field what many of you call God, Creator or Source. Just as you they are multidimensional beings existing on a vibrational continuum. Their lower bodies are more refined and their awareness is more aligned with what you refer to as Christ or Buddha consciousness. We could name all the other enlightened beings yet this would take a while just mentioning the multitude of masters of Earth. There are less dense physical 3d Pleiadians operating here on Earth, most are 4th, 5th, 6th and 7th dimensional. Fourth dimensional Pleiadians reside in their hearts and have a great love for all Creation. The 5th dimensional Pleiadians have mastered the spoken word, love expressed for all Creation. The 6th dimensional Pleiadians see the Creator in all Creation including themselves; everything is consciousness and energy to them. The seventh dimensional Pleiadians have become one with God, Creator, Source. When you understand the chakras and energy centers of consciousness you can best understand the nature of evolution. 1st chakra is survival, 2nd is sexual or creational, 3rd is power, 4th is love felt, 5th is love expressed, 6th is God seen in all creation, 7th is I AM God.

The majority of your civilization is focused primarily on survival, sex and power. There has been a grand scheme or manipulation using fear and insecurity to hold you there. That spell has been broken many times on Earth although many fell back into the spell. Now humanity is again breaking that spell and moving into love and beyond.

Pleiadian organic ship stepping down in frequency. The ship has a symbiotic relationship with pilot.

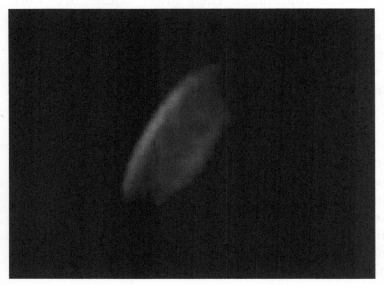

There was one known as Joshua bin Joseph, the Greeks called him Jesus which means son of Zeus. His prayer was accurately recorded when he said, "Beloved Father, let them become one as we are one." I would advise many on Earth to take him off the cross with the image of a bleeding man in pain and suffering used to create fear, guilt, unworthiness and control the masses. I would also advise humanity to realize his teachings were about love, unity, non-judgment and service. Find a new image more aligned with who he is. He is a loving, joyous, powerful manifesting God being with a great sense of humor. He often uses it to assist those who attune to him. Those on the plane of bliss do not entertain base emotions or communicate for very long with those who wish to do so. One has to rise to the occasion.

His physical body was a hybrid the seed of which came from an Ultra-dimensional named Gabriel combined with Mother Mary who held the original genetics from ancient Lyra. His soul was too powerful to inhabit a regular Earth body, he would have burned up the synapses. He came in from the plane of bliss where he already mastered judgment, loving detachment, any material need and the physical. He mastered the greatest of all tests; which was death itself. He was initiated within and studied many spiritual disciplines while maintaining his own personal God connection. He taught of an all loving all forgiving God the one consciousness that encompasses all consciousness on all planes and dimensions throughout the multiverse. The God within the spark that can be united into the full flame, at one-ment. This is what he meant when he said, "Be Still and Know Ye Are God, the temple is within, and Ye are all Gods." He was the exemplar Christ of what is within, a spell breaker as many others before and after him. His life was in balance. For those who have trouble with the archetype of Immaculate Conception, your scientists have already learned that DNA can be transferred by lasers, and water can be programmed with DNA. How simple would that be for an advanced civilization to impregnate and upgrade the DNA of a child? This is not uncommon and has been going on for a long, long time. It is part of the assistance on high in the awakening and healing process.

Chapter 11
Nature Spirits

Although there is myth and lore around Elves, Fairies, Gnomes, and other nature intelligences these stories all had origin in fact. To some this will all be dismissed yet to those who are awake and have opened to their sacred senses to them their world is as real as this world. Of course if you believe this world is real. This world owes its existence to the worlds above it for it is only a stepping down in frequency or vibration. There is a vibrational continuum worlds within worlds and these worlds are inhabited. They may be unseen to most but they do exist right alongside of us. There are places where the veils between worlds are very thin. This can also be created with spiritual practices and intention. We can raise our frequencies or go to places that are holding higher vibrations, sacred places to interact with these other worlds. The ECETI Ranch, Findhorn, Uluru, Machu Picchu, the Himalayas, the jungles, forests and even deserts, where the energies have been maintained, are all great opportunities to engage the higher realms.

Nature is one of the best places to awaken and heal. Working with the nature intelligences will greatly assist in any gardening for farming operation. Using natural organic methods along with daily attunement and intention to work with them will create miracle results. The gardens and farms flourish, there are less pests, and the food becomes highly charged and filled with minerals and vitamins if done properly. There is a saying, "Food should be your medicine," and knowing which foods to eat, their healing properties and growing them in a rich, highly charged and mineralized soil in conjunction with the nature spirits and moon cycles creates an unbelievable highly charged yield.

Many of the nature spirits have left civilized areas due to the toxic environment and consciousness of most humans. The psychic turbulence drives them away. It is time to welcome them back, align with them, cleanup our environments on every level. The Masters and Angelic kingdoms are all in alignment with the nature spirits. It is man/woman that is out of sync. Whenever you go out into nature honor them, invite them into your camp and remember it is not really your camp, they were there first. It is time to bring back the harmony, heaven on Earth and this means working with the nature intelligences, honoring their space rather than forcing our unconscious will upon them.

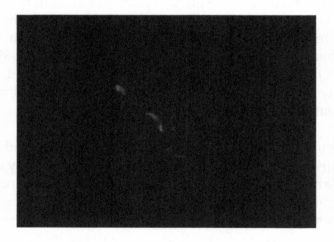

Fairy Spirit

Chapter 12

Bigfoot

At the height of the Nature kingdom is Big Foot or Sasquatch. Some refer to it as Yowie. I can only speak from my own experience concerning Big Foot, yet there are so many stories in our area, it is hard not to mention them. Skamania County in Washington State has the most credible verified sightings than anywhere in the world. In fact there is legislation protecting them. Most of the locals in Trout Lake, Washington have either had personal sightings or know of a relative or friend who has had an encounter. The Native Americans all know about the Big Foot nation and consider it a spiritual experience to encounter one. Legend has it if Big Foot appears to you it is a good sign. You must have good energy. They are also very sensitive and curious beings. The Elders say they bring messages about getting back to the land and spirit. I have had several encounters, many in the dream world, some up close and personal in this world. I had a very old silver one come now and then with younger ones at his side he was teaching. I saw a female 50 feet away. She was distraught and moaning due to being separated from her daughter. I believe that is the only reason I got so close to her. I had my hands out showing I was unarmed and sent her the telepathic message I was there to help. We sat there staring at each other. She was sitting on a log with small bushes in between us. She finally stood up and walked erect towards the forest across a wash. I had full vision of her and she smiled and nodded. I received the message thanks, but no thanks. It seemed clear they don't trust humans. I am sure they have good reasons. The odd thing about that encounter is she dematerialized before she reached the forest. In my experience it showed clearly they have the ability to move in and out of this dimension. I came across a large male near a waterfall with a friend of mine. He made it very clear we were encroaching on his territory by stomping and breaking limbs. I returned to the area and left apples and a banana, meditated and apologized. He took the apples and banana along with giving us a blessing, it felt like forgiveness. It felt as if he was very appreciative we dealt with him with honor and respect.

There have only been two stories I have heard where Big Foot acted aggressively yet it was not without provocation. One story was on the Yakama Reservation where they were logging in the higher elevations encroaching on their area. The large males picked up 50-gallon oil drums full of diesel and tossed them like toys on top of the portable cabins. They also picked up massive iron chokers and tossed them hitting the skidders and tractors disabling them. The Elders came, stopped the logging and told everyone they have to spend the next two weeks in prayer asking forgiveness. Another story was about a hunter who took a shot at two Big Foot. The male began howling and came down after the hunter. The hunter ran with his dogs far ahead down the mountain leaving everything behind including his gun. When he returned with others to retrieve his camp gear he found his gun twisted into a pretzel.

The funniest story was one I was personally involved in. It concerns a juvenile who likes to prank people at ECETI. His name is Dlaki, according to other spirit sources. Many have encountered him yet he only shows himself to certain people. I was present for one encounter with Clyde Lewis of Ground Zero, a talk show international in scope. It airs right before Coast to Coast having as much

58

if not more affiliates. Dlaki decided to run right up to Clyde, skid to a stop, smile and then take off through the orchards. It really turned Clyde upside down for a while. He said no one would believe him and decided not to talk about it on the air. He was doing a UFO and paranormal investigation at ECETI and was blown away already with the UFO and orb activity being documented. He had his engineer monitor all known satellites proving without a shadow of a doubt the UFOs were exactly that, unidentified flying objects. The Big Foot experience was over the top for him. Later in the week I took pictures of the tracks Dlaki left in the south pasture. Upon having that physical evidence Clyde decided to tell his story.

We need to honor, respect and preserve the habitat of the remaining Big Foot. Follow the lead of Skamania County and pass legislation to protect them. Anyone shooting a Big Foot should be prosecuted for murder. The DNA samples show clearly they are more human than ape. They evolved in nature adapting to their environment verses destroying the environment to suit the needs of modern man. There is one more thing I would like to add concerning all the Big Foot shows on TV. There is a Native American saying. "The only way you will find Big Foot is if Big Foot decides to find you." In other words unconscious people will search in vein.

Track left by Dlaki, juvenile Big Foot. Notice hinged foot not like human foot.

Chapter 13
Orbs, Apparitions and Shadow Beings

There are some beautiful movies and books about orbs. I was in Orbs the Veil is Lifting. A documentary with Randy and Hope Meade, which covers the subject in depth. I am writing this chapter due to the constant inquiries concerning the subject. There are many different types of orbs. They come in every size shape and color. The geometric patterns and colors often define who they are, where they come from and their main function. When we understand our own multidimensional nature we understand the nature of orbs. We have a physical body along with bodies of a more subtle nature all the way back to the source. The closer the energy or spirit bodies are to the physical the stronger the adherence to form. Eventually you become an orb with 360 degree vision and the ability to traverse dimensions. Orbs are a more unlimited version of the body and the laws of physics change as you move up the vibrational continuum.

James with Golden Light Eagle, leaving his body as an orb.

The colors that define the nature and abilities or main focus of the orbs range from brilliant to murky. The murky colors or darker colors often point to a clearing being necessary. Red is a highly volatile energy. It is a warriors' energy, murky red means it is time to do clearings. Orange is life energy, yellow often represents intellect, green is healing energy, blue represents love and wisdom, pink divine love often feminine, violet represents transmutation, and purple a high degree of spiritual adeptness. In many cases orbs are a projection of consciousness. Advanced beings have the ability to project themselves as an orb to guide, heal and observe. This includes spiritually and technologically advanced off-worlders. Mary often appears as a blue orb expanding into an apparition. There is a blue form of her preceding her manifestation. Quan Yin will appear as a column of orbs before she materialize.

Orbs appearing before Quan Yin materialized.

Quan Yin photo left painting on right.

Many warrior spirits like Konar, Rama etc. often appear as very large red spheres of light. Some beings can change their energies according to what is necessary. Your aura changes according to what you are engaging, this is similar to the light beings. Many of the nature spirits will appear, as orbs first then as you gain their trust will manifest in a lower body taking a form. There is nothing to fear about orbs if they take a dark or murky color in means it is time to do a clearing. When it comes to shadow beings when they appear again it signals it is time to maintain your own self authority, call on your representative of source or Creator and do a clearing. The clearing technique is at the end of the book. There are goat headed beings that like to press people down on their beds immobilizing them. Old Hags, Men with large black hats, even malevolent ETs. I have even seen combinations of ETs and astral or demonic beings. This is high level stuff most will never encounter these. Part of the path to enlightenment is experiencing these entities and learning how to deal with them. There is a spiritual war underway. As for mentioned the closer you get to nirvana, "enlightenment" the more the demons rear their ugly heads.

Man praying to the orbs.

Orbs responding to his prayer.

Arcturian orbs appearing at ECETI conference

Orbs during conference.

Chapter 14
Uluru and Kata Tjuta

On my trip to Uluru and Kata Tjuta Australia with Peter and Solrita with ECETI Australia, I had many experiences some of which I had to receive the counseling of a local Elder to understand. Brilliant golden ships flew over Uluru while sky watching along with the local parrots, eagles and ravens. I also connected with 5th dimensional Grandmothers, women in the 5th dimension who were desperately trying to lift the original people, the aboriginals in the 3rd many of which had given up hope. The Star Nations agreed to help them in their endeavor. This was pretty normal for us but what blew my mind were the 9 foot tall giants that appeared to me. They walked like a being we would refer to as Pan, had close shaved hair on their heads with a widows peaks. They were carrying a rack of feathers on their backs. Having absolutely no reference points to understand who these being were, I consulted a local Elder named Allen and his nephew affectionately known as Pancake. Both were excellent musicians, one with the guitar the other with a Didgeridoo. When I asked Allen if he had ever heard of these being his eyes lit up and said you saw the Junabi. I am spelling the name of these beings the best I can because aboriginal language is unwritten.

They have legends of what we would call Big Foot, little people and strange lights. This being seemed like a relative of what many would call Pan. These two enormous and muscular beings seemed to be on a mission. I was told they were like enforcers or clean-up crews for the outback. I would hate to be on the wrong side of them. I have had many experiences with other worldly beings completely outside the box. Only after I do research do I find out these beings actually do exist and have a recorded history. Just as in meeting the Feline beings I had no reference points until I did the research finding them replete throughout history. I cannot leave this topic without mentioning some of the aboriginal people we meet. Like the Native Americans they were extremely persecuted. Although much of this has stopped and has been acknowledged in what is known as Sorry Day it is not enough. There is a major reconciliation that has to happen. We felt the persecution while being there, it is psychometrized into the land. An underlying deep sadness. There needs to be a major heartfelt ceremony followed by deeds to clear this energy. It can't be swept under the rug. The nature spirits will eventually clean this up through earth changes using the elements of earth, fire, water and air. This may not fare well for the inhabitants of those lands. There are also the tortured and abused spirits there still attached to the land. We did our part while being there but it is far from what is necessary.

Chapter 15
Bilocation Experiences

I can speak about this subject from personal experience. Whereas these higher dimensional beings for the most part can bi-locate anywhere and anytime depending on the rules of their dimension the phenomena is pretty standard with some Yogis, Lamas, Shamans and Monks of the third dimension. There are many photos of masters appearing and disappearing, in some you can see right through them when meditating. I can speak of my own experiences the first one was in the dead of winter. I was meditating after a Self Mastery class and two of my students were in Mexico. Upon going into deep meditation I pondered the idea on how I could sure use some warm waters to swim in and how nice it would be to join them. I drifted off as if I were in a dream. In the dream I connected with my students, had lunch with them went for a swim then awoke. What was strange is I felt really refreshed with a bit of a sunburn for which I had no explanation. When the students returned from their trip they told me what a surprise it was to see me there. They spoke of how we had lunch, and I even drank a beer with them (which was odd because I very seldom drink), then went swimming. I just smiled and said I thought that was a dream.

The second time I bi-located was while I was driving from The Dalles, Oregon to Beaverton, Oregon to teach another Self Mastery Class. It is over an hour drive with no traffic. I had a disc out in my back and was praying on the way for healing to help me make this drive a little more comfortable. Fifteen minutes later I was in Beaverton at the house where I was going to teach the class. I was helping a friend remodel his house in The

Dalles and I left at 8 am in the morning only to reach there fifteen minutes later. The woman who owned the house did not believe me when I said I left at 8 am so she called the friend in The Dalles. He did not believe I was at her house, and said it was impossible. The next bilocation event was while driving with a German Physicist, Max in a Ryder truck full of healing technology equipment. We left LA and 6 hours later were in Eugene Oregon, which is impossible being a 17 hour trip especially with a large truck that bogged down on the slightest hill. We both looked at each other and said, "No way, do you remember anything... missing time, intervention, anything?" We both just accepted it considering the fact events like this were really nothing new. On the way down to LA we had an encounter with a large plane that was buzzing us. At one point I saw the landing gear of the plane coming right at the front window of the truck barely missing us. I asked my German friend if he knew what was going on and he said yes they want to see us in the ditch. Luckily we continued with the game of chicken ending after a couple more passes. Okay, back on the subject of bi-location. There were several times I would go out of body to meet with masters in the higher dimensions. There were times I ended up on ships both physically and out of body. There is technology that makes this possible yet for some the technology is not necessary. They can appear whenever and wherever they want just by willing it. It all depends on who is at both ends of the experience. The higher dimensional beings can appear as an orb with 360 degree vision. They can inspire, assist and send healing energies as well as clarity for those who initiate the experience. There is a sequence of photographs that show this experience taken by one of the volunteers at ECETI. My body is solid in the first photo, turns into energy, then a couple of lines of energy followed by a golden orb all in sequence.

A series of pictures were taken of Kan, a master teacher and monk from Japan, where he dematerializes then bi-locates. There have been a few taken as I leave my own body eyes closed on the physical body then eyes open on the body moving up and out. Many of my students have been photographed dematerializing. It is a natural process and not to be feared as long as one learns how to heal unseen negative influences and can maintain their own self-authority.

Kan dematerializing during rainbow body meditation

Notice eyes are closed in bottom body, open in upper
body.

Chapter 16
The Unseen War In The Heavens

There are many witnesses to flashes in the skies followed by loud booming noises. Some witnesses have seen light ships in the heavens while closer to Earth other ships were going up to engage the light ships. Some light ships were coming down to engage the regenerate ETs. There is Universal Law and agreements some of which have expiration dates. To fully understand what is happening in the heavens one has to know the real history of Earth. As we said earlier the Earth was colonized many times by different Star Nations. Andromedan, Sirian, Pleiadian, Orion Council of Light, Arcturian, Lyrian as well as other off worlders came to the Earth with the Pleiadians as the main force of these groups. Your moon was once a great Terra Forming ship; which was involved in this process. You once had two moons, then no moon, then one again. These Terra Formers were benevolent peaceful scientists; great geneticists and biologists who specialized in creating what some refer to as Edens.

The original plan was to create heaven on Earth (as above, so below), a place where beings could reach the height of evolution in the physical. Due to splits and disagreements the experiment was not a success. Lower evolved souls began to incarnate which created power struggles, hierarchies, and divisions. This also opened the door to great wars and cataclysms due to the misuse of technologies and natural cycles they no longer could control. Lesser evolved beings, Grey and Reptilian factions regenerate groups of a predatory and parasitic nature declared all-out war conquering the peaceful unprepared consortium. Over time the consortium has grown, evolved, became even more powerful and now are returning to reset the Earth on its original intent. Agreements were reached with the regenerate ETs who have not honored these agreements and now time and a half is over. Those regenerate ETs who refuse to end their controlling; manipulating tyrannical ways must leave or suffer dire consequences.

These regenerate predatory and parasitic ETs are the ones the humans of the same nature call upon for power over others in dark rituals within their elitist hierarchies. Many of the International bankers, some of the royals, political and religious leaders and corporate heads are influenced (if not fully taken over) by these entities. They are but a shell losing all personal power and soul connection, which is the God connection. As we said the mind in which you seek is the mind in which you connect. It truly is on Earth as it is in Heaven. A heavenly consciousness with heavenly deeds creates heaven on Earth. A hellish consciousness with hellish deeds creates hell on Earth.

With the end of the Iron Age or Kali Yuga and due to the alignment with Sirius, Alcyon and galactic plane the days of the regenerates are fast coming to a close. Their puppets, Earth humans known as the tyrannical elite will also find themselves in dire straits. When those in the unseen are exposed and removed those in the seen, puppets of the regenerates will lose their protection and suffer the karmic backlash as well as exposure as to who they are and what they have done. The masks and facades are all coming down. The old consciousness and energy grids are rapidly diminishing and the new grids of love, joy peace and freedom are taking their place. You are going to see great changes concerning government, religious and business institutions. Those that cannot adapt and transform to the new grid will fall by the wayside. The many world theory is correct and this world is merging with the higher aspect of itself due to the alignment with Galactic plane and the vibrational lifting, the awakening and healing of humanity and the Earth. The old world is imploding, its grids are falling apart. It is like the cosmic glue that held it all together is failing. The good news is there is a new world to take its place we just have to resonate and become frequency specific with it.

Chapter 17
Dancing with the Archons

Who are the Archons? In the Nag Hammadi, a book that has been unaltered throughout time, the Archons are defined as a group of beings that are very controlling, masters at manipulation who inspire and feed off of negative experiences, and the energies they generate. They can easily influence fear, anger, jealousy, disharmony, war, actions disempowering and even enslaving the masses. They have been referred to as other names by other cultures, fallen angels, djinn, demons, lower astral beings, regenerate ETs, some greys, reptilian or serpent beings etc. When one is on the path of enlightenment the Archons will rear their ugly heads and come through every conceivable opening or way to keep you under their control. They will come through friends, family, bosses, lovers and almost every agency on the planet. They are masters at derailing your spiritual evolution. Many have willingly chosen to serve their needs, some by fear, some by ignorance, some through material attachment and some by choosing to entertain their baser emotions of the ego. Love, joy, individual freedom and prosperity, unity consciousness, and nature herself are the enemies of the Archons. Service to others with impeccable integrity over service to self, also keeps them at bay.

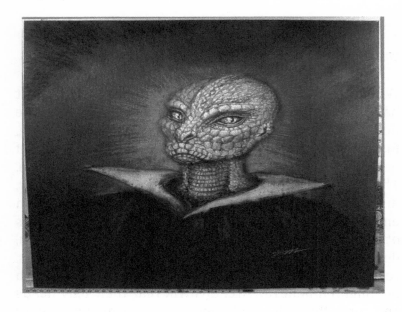

Reptilian being, one picture of many varieties.

Those who are unconscious, self-absorbed, self-centered or sociopaths living a life of disunity with material attachments or the need for acceptance and approval through material acquisition or outer appearances are easy pray for the Archons. Those under the influence of the Archons depending on the influence will find this information very uncomfortable some to the point where they will not be able to read any further. If you are feeling put off by this message odds are there is something in your life you need to let go of or change.

As this is written the major powers of Earth are controlled by the Archons and their influence is felt throughout all society. The more hierarchal, departmentalized and often technological separate from nature the more society is often controlled by the

Archons. The more self empowered, unified, and natural the less the influence. This is a generalization of course not all technology fits into this pattern, technology can be used for positive or negative depending on who is directing the technology. When one is conscious and aware of this they can actually use technology to empower and awaken the masses yet one cannot be in denial of being under the influence of the Archon program. It takes a real adept to avoid contamination and mental enslavement. On the Earth now the major use of technology is the war industry. There are also the pharmaceutical companies, which often create dependencies on harmful drugs, and lesson the health of the individual. The chemical companies also play a major role in the dumbing down and poisoning of the masses. There are other industries developing methods of spying upon, conditioning and controlling the masses. Your television and other broadcasted frequencies are good examples. Reason this how many people are willing participants in creating, utilizing, and misusing technology in ways that go against basic human rights and universal law. How many people use technology in ways that are harmful, enslaving, invading ones right to privacy? Mind manipulation or controls outside of universal law are serving the Archons or what some refer to as the Beast.

Despite denial and intellectually dismissing ones actions and how they affect others such as it's my job, it's for God and country, I have to feed my family pay my bills etc. these are all reasons for doing what one knows in the soul to be out of alignment with universal law or Right Livelihood. If you are a part of the Archon network the network owns you. The way this comes about is through the baser attitudes emotions or the first three chakras;

which represent survival, sex and power. The Archons own these first three chakras and choosing a life of materialism seeking acceptance and approval though outer appearances or material acquisition is how they trap the unconscious. The Archons know people will sell their souls for fame, trinkets, bobbles and little green pieces of paper. This is why when you climb the ladder of success you often find at the top of that ladder it gets darker, more complicated and completely out of alignment with universal law, soul and spirit or right livelihood.

You will find at the top often those in the political, business and religious institutions are often people with a total disconnect to their souls. They have no real moral guidance or character, compassion, remorse and have often reached a level of narcissism, upon where base logic and critical thinking cannot apply. They always have hidden agendas, use and lust for more power over others, their need and greed is unbridled with absolutely no remorse on how their actions negatively impact others or nature. You are a pond a stepping-stone to use for personal gain. You can expect their actions to be the exact opposite of their words. They are the master liars, manipulators and double speak is their language. The Archons can come through anyone in the matrix anytime, anywhere even those closest to you who fall into the Archon matrix and wreak havoc in your life. Unfortunately this is the state of consciousness of not all but the majority of the leadership in government, religious and business institutions. It is not just on the higher levels this is acted out, many have become so programmed even on the lowest levels of what society calls the have-nots, because many have been brainwashed into believing the haves are happy friendly loving people of high character. When they get to the top they realize they had more of what is of true value at the bottom. The fame, bobbles, trinkets and wealth are mere carrots on a stick to get them to climb the ladder of degradation.

This ladder of degradation has many rungs and to understand how it works one must be separated from their heart and soul even what some would call base logic and critical thinking. Although the ladder gives you the illusion of climbing upward in fact spiritually and according to soul evolution it is a downward spiral. To climb the ladder you have to give up something. Let's say a little lie or act that may not be in the highest and best good of humanity and the Earth. You have to give up impeccable integrity. The next rung has a few more lies and actions that make it a little harder to maintain the connection to soul and spirit. As one climbs the ladder there are more lies and actions with the intellect stepping in and validating why it is necessary. I need the job, there are things I need usually programmed through advertisements and social programming. Then you have to do things you would normally not do to get these things, I have a family to feed, it is for God and Country etc. The latest is it is for security and to preserve freedom yet in truth the actions create the opposite effect. As you move up the ladder you are given shiny badges, positions of power, wealth and the image of success. Yet all the while you are incapable of realizing the ladder of success is the Archon ladder; which ends in failure in total ruin becoming totally disconnected with soul and spirit living among others void of soul and spirit, no love, joy, bliss disconnected from source. What you think will make you happy is the program you bought into forgetting that love, joy, bliss, even abundance is you natural state and you did not even have to get on the illusionary Archon ladder of success. Your world becomes a material prison; a fake world based on acceptance and approval outside of self propped up by an increase in material acquisition then more investment into outer appearances. Your world becomes the one sold to you and programmed by the Archons, the American Dream. Did you know why they call it a dream? You have to be asleep to believe in it.

In higher evolved spiritually and technologically advanced civilizations, their technology always serves their people, their leadership is chosen by their spiritual advancement and history of real service to their people and their environment. Not the fabricated stories of service by the lame stream media with false titles, prizes and events. Yes we enjoy the puns. Your leadership is bought, selected and groomed to control the masses in most cases the direct result of which is the condition of your society and environment. Now here is the big reality check. If your leadership was truly elected by the people and in service to the people how on Earth could society and the environment be in such disarray, such disharmony, why is there so much disease, pain and suffering? Why is there such a gross uneven dispersal of wealth? This is 2016 is it not? Compared to what is possible you are living in the dark ages.

Chapter 18

Bingo, did the light just go on?

How does a hierarchy fit into unity consciousness and service to others? If you are not programmed by this false reality why do you participate in it? On any level, remember impeccable integrity? What you knew as a child before the programming is the real wisdom and it took years of programming, abuse and "education" to talk you out of it. How many can break through the illusion, see the ladder for what it is? Very few! Observe what happens when you try to take the ladder of success away from them. They have to fall over the wall or drink enough sour wine before they are ready to release the ladder. Often it is too late, due to years and years of lies, actions and conditioning clouding their connection to soul and spirit, to get back to the innocence of at one-ment they had as a child. This is why it is said you must become like children to enter the kingdom of heaven. You must be free of the lies, actions, programming what some call ignorance and karma and choose right thinking, right action, right living in harmony with each other and nature. Let us not forget doing so with impeccable integrity. Your connection to soul and spirit depend on it.

Chapter 19

When Love Goes Dark

There is a phenomenon that happened three times in my life yet with the most recent mate I finally mastered the experience, or I would like to think so. It is a very hard lesson and challenge, which tests you to the depths of your soul. I am sharing this to help others who are being challenged in the same arena to let them know they are not alone. In each relationship there were common denominators. These lovers were usually abandoned or abused by their father in some cases both parents may have abandoned or abused them. There is often rape or molestation in their past. Sometimes a history of drug abuse; which includes medical psychotropic drugs given to them by psychologists or psychiatrists trying to mask the situation. This opens the doors to other unseen negative influences making matters worse. Many are the byproducts of covert operations creating sex slaves or agents to be used in honey traps. Most will be unaware of their childhood blocking out such traumatic events yet these events sabotage their relationships if allowed to go unhealed. Because of this they have the classic love hate relationships. These are relationships where they want to love and punish at the same time projecting the cause of the childhood pain and suffering on an unsuspecting lover. They also cannot go to any depth of love, will sabotage the relationship before it can go to any depth due to fear of being vulnerable and getting hurt again. They can change their heart like they change their shoes. It was a classic fem fatale program in my experiences yet there was a lot more to the story then just childhood wounds and traumas. I kept soul searching, looking for childhood trauma in my own life that would attract these events yet I had a wonderful childhood other than the adjustment of the soul to a denser vibration remembering from where I came. The mirror effect just did not apply, yet again according to the Essene teachings there are 7 different kinds of mirrors.

The Hindu saying the closer you get to Nirvana the more the demons rear their ugly heads fits perfect into this category. The demons or let us say archons in this case were of a different sort. They were serpent beings, a very aggressive venomous lot very powerful and dealing with them takes real Self Mastery. They hook you through the first three chakras then use those closest to you to slam you through the heart. Your lover, friends, family anyone close to you with an unhealed past, trauma or a week mind are easy prey and used as tools to take you out mentally, emotionally and through the astral body. I watched these energies descend upon my mate not once but three separate times after which all hell broke out. They became cold hearted, cruel, and indifferent despite all appeals to their heart, prayers, reasoning, and clearings of negative influences. They had become someone else overnight, leaving you gut punched and heart broken. When you have a deep soul and spirit connection with people this makes matters worse because the archons begin their work at a very young age. If there was a greater plan to incarnate and unify from the highest levels bringing heaven to Earth the archons will do their best to sabotage that plan from birth on. Inducing trauma, negatively inspiring parents, family, friends and lovers to inflict trauma does this. The purpose of this is separate people from their etheric body, the heart and soul connection leaving only their astral body and ego which can be used by the archons. They are parasitic feeders residing in the astral levels.

They use people to do their bidding. They lock people into their astral body and ego separate them from soul and spirit keeping them from the divine plan, arrangements made on high through trauma. If it is not enough for parents to deal with their own dysfunction these beings know at birth, which individual is going to be a threat to their empire and they are not bound by time distance and space. They will use the parent's dysfunctions against the children.

When this happens in your personal relationships all you can do is cut the cords, do ceremonies to close the door wall off these energies and make space between the people who have chosen to allow the archons in due to a lack of awareness, past life and childhood trauma. This does not mean giving up on them it means pray and heal from a distance. They will have their train wreck, their karma will come swiftly all you can do is allow them to experience what universal law has for them, the reaction to their actions. The healing process from here on out for them will be wrought with hard lessons, along with the purging effects of allowing these entities to take hold. This often includes the purging of anger, sadness, deep emotional releases, illnesses, lack of energy, even vomiting and diarrhea as the entities are driven out. These negative influences as well as the wounds, traumas, and programs that do not align with soul and spirit are being vibrationally lifted accelerated and healed. It is just a matter of choosing how hard the lesson will be to get the ego to surrender to spirit. Universal Law is pressing hard on the Earth whereas once one could temporarily get away with these negative alignments; choices and actions the reactions now are almost instantaneous.

When I say chosen there are always choices, actions, and the breaking of universal laws; which allow these negative influences to enter. A person of high integrity and of strong moral character who has chosen to heal would have the discernment and the love and respect of others to not engage in negative choices and actions. They would honor their mates, not betray the trust despite the wounds and traumas of the past and a relationship bound by spirit as well as agreements and arrangements made on high are honored. They would seek healing and own what was surfacing within them without projecting and blaming others for their emotions or lack thereof. When I say the lack of emotions what I am referring to is the lack of love within self, seeking it outside of self. Those who seek outside of self are easily manipulated by the Archons; which can send energies to inspire unhealthy connections derailing ones spiritual path. They can make you think you are in love with someone energizing the first three chakras, survival, sex and power in which the decisions are made from the programs within the ego. The heart soul and spirit usually have a different agenda a different path yet many fool themselves into a shallow superficial love due to the influences of the activations in the first three chakras. Their decisions are based on need be it emotional or physical mistakenly thinking it will bring security. There is no security in not aligning with soul and spirit and fulfilling the arrangements and agreements of soul and spirit.

In some cases due to all the dysfunction and negative influences the foundation is missing, the examples of a healthy relationship were never there and some don't even know due to their reference points what is proper and just. They live according to the images given to them by their father, mother and their environment. They are molded by the experiences of their childhood even if those images and experiences were completely dysfunctional and out of alignment with universal law.

Focusing on the positive, gratitude and service to others over self-service helps diminish the effects of an unhealed past. Becoming the observer, monitoring ones attitudes and emotions being responsible and accountable for ones choices and actions is a priority towards healing and keeping the peace. Without healthy reference points many do not even know where to start or have the courage to admit to the damage done by their dysfunctional past. In the case of a sociopath there is no remorse or desire to be accountable or take responsibility for their choices and actions they just move on until universal law drops the hammer on them. This keeps the door open for these unseen negative influences and until addressed and healed we cannot expect anything else other than toxic, wounded ego driven relationships with the same end.

When the serpent beings jump in what you will see is the aura turn grey to dark. The disconnect below the etheric body is like a grey or dark bubble surrounding the body, which is why the expression "they turned to the dark side". There is often a black ball below the heart. It sometimes looks like a ball of worms or small snakes clairvoyantly.

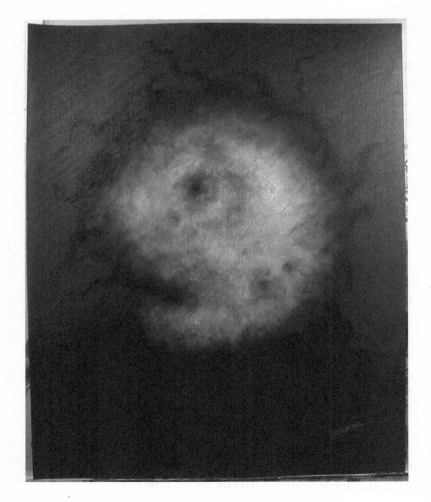

Black disc with what looks like snakes.

I saw a black cord connected to a black disk between my x and the one who was manipulating her. The disk was an opening to another dimension, a serpent energy along with reptilians and tall greys. A dark ritual, a bonding ceremony without her knowledge, created these dark psychic bonds and the disk like void connecting to the archon world. The black disk through this cord was tied into the sexual and power centers holding her down from the higher centers of awareness. At the time though aware of what happened seeing it clairvoyantly and of course getting several second opinions by some of the best seers I did not have the wisdom or the power to clear it. This has changed and with the new energies coming in there are new resources, the benevolent protectors of the Gods. The 7th dimensional Lion beings assisted in this clearing.

In the worst-case possession scenarios their eyes turn black, this is usually the case with those who practice dark rituals during the ritual. It also shifts when they feel threatened. Out of desperation some turn to dark manipulative sorcery to save their relationships using whatever method possible rather than healing themselves or taking responsibility. Controlling and manipulating the other is what they in error believe is the easier path. Problem is it is only temporary and does not fit into the awakening and healing process. Those who are not clairvoyant will feel a gut and heart wrenching energy. Connecting with the heart of ones mate from here on out can be deadly for now there is something ominous in between you and your mate, friends and family whoever has been afflicted. When this happens no amount of love, reason, appeal to the heart matters the person you once loved is gone. The loving, glowing God or Goddess you were once with became the opposite. They will come up with many shallow superficial reasons for their actions, refuse to take responsibility and to add salt to the wound will blame you for the very things they themselves did or are doing.

They will find all kinds of reasons to validate their actions never looking at the actions themselves. It is crazy making yet that is the goal, to drive you away from love, joy, bliss your own soul and spirit connection. Most won't even remember what they did it is like a drunk the next morning oblivious to what they did the night before.

These serpent beings as well as the entire archon network have absolutely no compassion, care nothing for your wellbeing and in fact desire just the opposite, your physical, mental, emotional and spiritual demise inflicting as much pain and suffering as possible. This is very hard for some people to accept. Those they have possessed are often not even aware of their actions and how they affect others or why they too have so much pain suffering and sorrow in their own lives. These serpents feed off the anger, pain and sorrow. A good example of the serpent or archon network is the military. How else could you destroy villages, towns, even countries killing families, innocent men, women and children? This includes pregnant women and babies leaving a toxic wasteland all for the corporate profit with no remorse? Certain military and other malevolent agencies engage in remote influencing. They can project feelings that are not really yours due to agreements with the darker forces, often engage in black magic, technological voodoo against the so called enemy or people they want to manipulate.

The adepts in the dark arts can create bonds and spells; which can easily influence the un-awakened. They can even do this through technology due to a little help from the Greys and Reptilians. There is an old saying you become what you sleep with and this in many cases is how these energies hook you. If you are part of the archon network you are a pond for these influences. Why do you think so many soldiers are committing suicide? They cannot live with these energies, what they have done and see it as the only way out. Their mates, friends and families can feel the influences of trauma of war and the archon network; which creates further divisions. There is another way and that is to forgive your-self, gain the wisdom from the experience and realign with soul and spirit. Make restitution, fight the archons, expose them, show what is really happening in these wars and actions; which cause so much pain and suffering and diminish freedom. Focus as well on who is profiting from them. As we said those giving the orders for these wars all the way to the top are in the archon network. The war and disease profiteers, the controllers, those enslaving humanity through dependency in their lust for power and wealth all are a part of this network.

If you encounter beings such as these the good news is you must be a threat, a powerful spirit close to awakening or enlightenment. They usually do not go after those who are disconnected from soul and spirit or asleep. It is an opportunity to shine your light brighter and transcend any fear or doubt. The sheeple are no threat to them. They only use the un-awakened as ponds within the matrix. We have to thank these ponds, forgive them and give thanks for bringing us the lessons and awareness of what we don't want in our lives. We have to hold a sacred space and allow them in when they have chosen to heal and awaken. This is tough love and love of self demands setting firm boundaries.

Having encountered this energy more than once I finally found the solution. There is one group of beings that can deal with these serpent beings. As I mentioned earlier

95

they are the seventh dimensional Lion Beings known as the protectors of the Gods. Although many others can assist in protection sometimes driving them off, they seem to come back. These benevolent protectors known in India as Maat, Narshringa or Narasimha, in Egypt known as Sekhmet - some call them the Pashat. They are powerful allies when dealing with these energies. They will remove them from your space, remove them from those close to you but they cannot interfere in choice and action or free will. If those who were afflicted choose to continue down the path that led them to be possessed by these entities you can't help them. Although it seems incredibly unwise even insane to walk back into the den of vipers, the dysfunctional relationships rather than choose a different path many do. It is like a heroin addiction, what is known and in error they believe there is safety there as long as they too support the dysfunction. The programming is too deep and only when they hit rock bottom or the wall will they realize how empty their lives have become, where they led themselves, how they were seduced and misled. The disconnect with soul and spirit is always a dead end - yet the wounded ego drives them over and over down the same road.

The American dream needs to be seen for what it is an enslaving manipulation into servitude. It is an outward distraction from the God/Goddess within. Unfortunately for some it may be too late. It is hard for those of heart to watch this and not jump in and try to save them, reason with them, tell them there is nothing for them at the end of the path yet these are the hooks that take you down the path with them. Sometimes the most loving compassionate thing you can do is allow them their journey, the hard lessons and create space in some cases for someone else. This time with the wisdom gained from the experience, releasing the past and to choose a little wiser on the next go around.

Chapter 20

Never Give Up

Never give up on those you love yet love yourself enough to set any necessary boundaries. See the Godself within them, project the truth of their being. Always remember there are those who have been observing us for thousands of years never giving up, holding us in the light. One relationship is a mere blip in the history of an eternal soul. In my last relationship we spent 37 lifetimes together 14 of them I tried to pull her out of 3d attachment, ritual abuse and heal the wounds and traumas. She had also helped me as a cripple in one life I am aware of probably others. To this day I hold the memories of the times she was a glowing angel and the passion between us sending healing and clearing the unseen negative influences daily. We never know what is transpiring by looking at the surface yet sending love always helps. I was told by a beautiful being, Isis one day that you cannot stop loving, love is the only way out. We can't close our hearts, we can choose to whom and where we direct our attention and energies. We are still held accountable for choices and actions life after life outside of universal law. It is up to everyone to open to the energies, heal and clean up their messes. The chapter is still open for a different ending yet only when those afflicted realize what really happened and are ready to take full responsibility for their choices and actions, not be a victim when the consequences of those choices and actions return and heal without blame and projection, when they fully commit to soul and spirit then and only then will it have a different ending. The Source and the Beautiful Many Saints Sages and masters rejoice in those who have the courage to heal, release the past and realign with soul and spirit. They are waiting in the wings we just have to ask and commit to the process. This includes the awakened ones on Earth who have chosen a path of service to God/Creator/Spirit the Omnipresent God throughout all creation.

Chapter 21
Moving On

We never know what a soul needs for completion. When choosing again be sure it is someone who is not obsessed with their outer appearances due to programming by the archon network, in need of acceptance and approval outside of self, insecure due to wounds and traumas of the past. Be sure they are not a part of or serving the network. Choose someone of strong moral character dedicated to living a spiritual path where honesty, loyalty and integrity are first and foremost as a way of life. Find someone obsessed with their inner awareness, their own personal God connection, some one free of the archon network, someone who is fully aware of the acceptance and approval of the God within. Then you will find peace and true security. The days of the wounded egos are coming to a close. With the new frequencies they do not have the luxury to continue business as usual. The universe and universal law will amplify and accelerate their learning process, deliver the lessons hard as they may be to get them back into alignment with soul and spirit. Even if that means leaving the body behind in the most stubborn cases. If we redirected our energies to our own awakening and healing, making our own personal God/Creator/Spirit connection the world would be a better place and we will eventually draw to us someone of like mind on the same path. There is always the choice to choose the path of the wounded ego with open doors to the archon network or heal aligning with soul and spirit honoring the agreements made from soul and spirit. You cannot choose the path for others that is up to them.

I had my dance with the serpent beings at a very early age. I just had my NDE a drowning were I returned to source and back. One afternoon I was meditating and a very powerful dark being descended into my body. I had tremendous power but I felt it was not love, joy or bliss it was power over others. If I allowed it to have its way tremendous wealth, power, fame all would have come to me yet it was at a price. The levels of love, joy, and bliss - my God connection - would diminish and I was not willing to give that up. I challenged it then the battle began. They do not like to be challenged which invokes an arrogant vengeance, a game of manipulation and promises. I knew right away I wanted this entity out of my space out of my body.

Serpent Being, Dark Overlord.

I called on the Father/Mother God, the I AM. I called upon Jesus, Mary every master, saint and sage I could think of. I said over and over I am the Living Christ. I was still outside of my body and it had control of my body. This went on all night long. Little by little I began to get control of my toes, fingers, then legs and arms though I was weak and cold not move them with any real strength. I continued to battle reaffirming I AM The Living Christ. This is my body given to me by God. In the wee hours of the morning I had enough control over my body to stand. I walked down to the beach and as the sun rose I walked into the water fully clothed. I knew the Sun rise and the salt water would end the battle and it did. I sat on the beach basically cursing the masters feeling abandoned.

I thought I had protection then I heard a voice within saying you did well my son. I again said I thought I had protection where were you. I recognized the voice and the energy. It was Joshua bin Joseph, "Jesus". He said this was your initiation. You had to go through it to know and understand the dark side. Now you have mastered it and you can help others knowing it is real. You will never forget this experience. I said "How do I know this is not just my imagination, all this is not just me going psycho, I want solid proof if I am going to continue". Just then I looked down and at my feet was a piece of sandstone, a perfect heart. I looked up and down the beach no other rocks or shells just sand. I could not intellectualize it away. I have kept this heart as a reminder of that day. It is part of enlightenment; an experience on the road to self-mastery to go through these initiations and the masters cannot do it for us. We have to become the Master eventually all they can do is inspire and assist as long as we are going forward in our own self-mastery.

Chapter 22
Tools for Healing Unseen Negative Influences

Healing is a must for all those who desire to operate in other realms of consciousness. You must maintain self - authority and control. If you are experiencing negative vibrations, they are either thought forms, limiting mental concepts, psychic bonds or discarnate entities (lost souls) in need of healing. They are bound to the earth vibration due to lower vibrational attitudes and emotions. Some are coercive and desire to manipulate or control. Love heals. Casting out only sends them to another place, another person. In all healings, remember that the ultimate power is love, god is love. It is the power of love that heals and lifts. We will give you the following steps to clear the energy.

1. Close your aura by visualizing a white or gold light around you.

2. Call upon your chosen cultural representative of God, be it Jesus, Buddha, Babaji, Mary, Mohammed, White Eagle or another one of the beautiful Many Christed Ones. The lord God of your being also works.

3. Tell the entities they are healed and forgiven, lifted and enlightened. (repeat if you feel it is needed)

4. Tell them that they are filled and surrounded with the Christ light and the Christ love (or the highest consciousness and energy available)

5. Ask that your chosen representative to take them to their perfect place and highest expression.

6. Ask that all negative thought forms, and limiting mental concepts be dissolved, and lifted into the light of truth.

7. Ask that all psychic bonds be severed, and close their auras to all but spirit of the highest vibration. Repeat this process until you feel clear. There may be more than one healing to do.

Remember that your word is very powerful, and what is spoken on their level manifests instantly. Many enlightened ones use this process before opening. It creates a clear and safe environment and it also lifts the one who is doing the healing. Intent is nine-tenths of the law! I would highly recommend practicing this healing method after reading about the archons and their ways. Often just mentioning them brings them into our awareness or opens doors to dealings with them in the past. Again enlightenment means to be in knowledge of both sides of the coin. Self Master means learning and using tools to maintain self-authority and the ability to clear ones energy and the energy around them.

Chapter 23
Help and the solution

The Good news is this archon network is falling apart. Those who align with it are going to be caught up in its downward spiral ending up in total collapse as the grid that supports it comes crashing down. Those of heart and soul dedicated to service and aligned with universal law, principles and understandings necessary for a healthy society and environment will prevail. Those in opposition or conflict with universal law will experience the hard lessons as karma is amplified and accelerated. Denial and being unconscious will not save one from the reactions to their actions or what some refer to as the great purification or cleansing.

There is a vibrational lifting, an awakening and healing in process. It is growing exponentially and now it is in hyper drive. This is due to natural planetary cycles and alignments, the alignment with Galactic Plane and higher dimensional forces. Everything must align with this process, either reconfigure, transform or collapse. There will be some that will physically collapse, have mental and emotional breakdowns, and some will have breakthroughs. It is all relative to their resistance. We must become frequency specific to the new Earth and align with universal law to continue on Gaia. To some it will be welcomed and met with an open mind and loving heart. Even the social, economic and physical Earth changes will be a welcomed event because they know it is necessary for Earth to continue to be the platform for life. They also know it is a sign of the awakening and demise of the archon network.

Earth has become infected with greed, tyranny and the belief in separation. This infection has reached epidemic proportions up to the highest levels and it gets darker the higher up the archon ladder one goes. You are being governed by predators and parasites along with malevolent AI technology. Your banksters, politicians, governments and their agencies, and military almost all governing bodies even on a local level have become infected. It is time for the good people within all these agencies and institutions to rise up, take a stand, refuse to engage in any actions that diminish freedom and are harmful to humanity and the Earth. These institutions and agencies are given the power to serve the people, not serve themselves, their Napoleonic complexes or the corporations. The vast majority of the people are good, do not want conflict, do not want harm to come to anyone and now is the time for the good people to rise. There is a great power and force behind you. It is said one on the side of God is the majority. What would happen if the majority chose to side with God and live according to universal law? Not the graven images of religions, the God of Love the omnipresent God, the Creator in all Creation living a life in harmony with each other and Nature. Now is a time of choosing and action.

The archon grid, the network will no longer be allowed. Those that serve it will meet the same demise. The days of tyranny are coming to a close. It is already in motion and soon the heavens will open to forces and legions beyond imagination. There is nothing to worry about from those who come on high. It is those on low who are already here that one needs to be aware of. Do not fear the heavens.

Chapter 24
The Grand Awakening

The grand awakening is not going to be done to you or for you it is going to be done through you. That is the nature of creation. The external follows the internal. There are those who understand this process and have full access to the creational energies while others have partial access depending on their spiritual evolution. Heaven on Earth is an internal process; it is allowing the source, God/Creator/Spirit to flow through you. It is attuning too the higher planes and dimensions, drawing upon them, awakening, remembering you divinity that creates Heaven on Earth. This also needs to be grounded in deed and action. We can't just talk the walk we need to walk the talk. Balance is the key.

Many speak of the right hand and left hand path. The right hand is self-serving, seeks power, notoriety, fame, wealth yet often this comes with a price. Many of these desires come from the ego - and with some a very wounded ego filled with trauma, childhood and past life. The desire for power over others is due to being overpowered in the past. The need for fame and notoriety comes from the need for acceptance and approval outside of self, acceptance and approval that was not given in childhood or again in past lives. It also comes from the disconnect with soul and spirit, from the God within that loves and approves of you beyond your wildest dream. It does not have an ego to judge yet action/reaction or karma will take care of choices and actions outside of universal law. The obsession for wealth is also coming from times of lack or the misperception of wealth establishing security and self-worth. How much gold, how many cars, and how many mansions does a person need to establish self-worth? Is there any security in obtaining wealth at the expense of others, the exploitation of nature? Universal law or karma in an immutable law and cannot be usurped. It can be lessened and cleared up however, through forgiveness and restitution, dharma, committing one's energy and resources to the awakening and healing process.

The left hand path is based on service to others, empowering others, humility, often associated with a life of poverty. While creating a lot of good karma the imbalance can hinder ones work not having the funds and materials necessary to complete ones mission. Many believe this world is an illusion, ignore the physical yet what is done in the physical weighs light or heavy on the soul. If you do not see the body as divine and ground heaven on Earth it will not ascend and turn into dust. We are not here to bail out and go to a higher dimension we came from the higher dimensions to create heaven on Earth. One does not ascend by leaving the body one ascends by bringing spirit fully present within the body. This creates a quickening an acceleration in mass eventually taking the body with you. Then you don't have to go through the birth canal to get another physical body.

I wish to impart a story for better understanding. A man went to the forest to leave society realizing all the ills of society to live a different path. He wanted to be at one with Nature, he did not want to take from Nature. The summer was great yet winter was soon to come upon him. He realized he needed wood to build his shelter yet did not want to take anything from the forest. He needed heat to survive the winters and store food yet he again did not want to take or hoard. He believed everything would be provided if he just became one with Nature. He felt he could find what he needed even in winter. It became colder and colder. He needed a warmer garment yet he did not want to kill anything. The foods he gathered for survival were diminishing as the seasoned changed. Soon the man found himself in a dilemma. No food, no warm clothing, no shelter.

After deep contemplation he realized the other animals all took from the forest yet they all gave to the forest each in their own way. He saw how the deer grazed on the grasses then fertilized the grasses eventually to become part of the cycle feeding a predator or feeding the soil upon their demise. The predators thinned the herds to weed out the sick and prevent over grazing. He realized he was out of balance. How could he take yet give as well. He realized he could take the trees where they needed thinning or dead trees while maintaining the forest. He realized he could thin the herd to meet his needs just as the predators because without weeding out the sick and with overpopulation the herd was weakened. He realized he could store food for winter as long as he left enough roots and seed behind to ensure another crop. He also realized other animals had their needs as well so was sure to not take more than was necessary and spread the roots and seeds creating abundance. Eventually he found balance his place in the forest. He also found his connection to the Creator within all Creation and his needs to sustain himself greatly diminished. He seemed to exist on and was supported by another force beyond the physical. He met a woman, had a child and passed on his ways and knowledge. The land was always in better shape than he found it when he left and by passing down the knowledge other generations followed in his footsteps. He acknowledge the creator in all creation, gave thanks for everything sharing his abundance. The balance he found, his gratitude and sharing opened the possibility of the creational energies to flow through him. From that point on he lacked for nothing. His offspring acknowledging his gratitude and sharing, the value of his wisdom made sure he was taken care of in his later years. In that lies true security.

His brother was a different story. He lusted for power and wealth at the expense of others and nature. He took without giving, exploited whoever and whatever he could. Because of his disrespect for others and life, life disrespected him eventually dying at an early age alone with his offspring fighting over what he left behind. All he had to take with him was his karma in the end. The legacy he left behind was a legacy of cold, imbalanced self-absorbed family and friends, no love, joy and their environment was toxic in many cases destroyed. These are the polarities now expressing on the Earth being amplified into ascension or demise. Our choices and actions determine our tomorrow.

As foretold, "The mind in which we seek, is the mind in which we connect." This is true in the seen and unseen. Making one's own personal God/Spirit/Creator connection and finding balance is the key. Right thinking, right feeling, right action will cure all the ills of society. Within everyone is a loving, joyous, powerful manifesting God/Goddess, the spark waiting to ignite into the full flame. The fuel is coming and the fuel is the pipe-line of soul and spirit activated on high from within. This is the destiny of Earth, we are at the crossroads and our choices and actions from here on out will determine our future on Earth and in the afterlife. What we do here on Earth weighs light or heavy on the soul and heavy souls end up in heavy places. The Earth will no longer be frequency specific to their vibration and they will not be allowed to incarnate again. She will have ascended to the next level. Those lineages and families you thought you would incarnate into again to maintain your power and wealth, they too will be gone for they as well are not frequency specific.

It is really quite simple. Everything has a vibration or frequency. Fear, guilt, anger, dishonesty, selfishness, jealousy, revenge, guilt, greed, unworthiness all have a very low vibration. Love, joy, bliss, service to the Creator in all Creation has the highest vibration or frequency. The more we release the past, awaken and heal focusing on love, joy, bliss and service the higher our frequency. The Earth is ascending, raising in vibration and frequency. We have to rise along with her. Resistance is futile and will only result in self-sabotage and self-defeat. Now is the time to choose the upward spiral into universal peace, brother/sisterly love, service to the Creator in all Creation, balance the path to ascension or the downward spiral ending in social, economic and environmental collapse. The lines have been drawn, the polarities are becoming stronger, everything is being revealed - no rock is being left unturned.

A new world is unfolding, the old world is collapsing. This is part of a natural cycle assisted by those on high to the very source itself. Time to get with the program your future here on Earth depends on it. For those who want nuts and bolts as proof to everything go to the hardware store. Your science has proven there are at least 11 dimensions and you can only measure less than one percent of the world in which you live. Why dismiss and ignore the other 99%. It is revealing itself in grand ways for those with open minds and loving hearts. Why separate yourself from the grandness that is you? You truly are a multidimensional being existing on a vibrational continuum; you have multidimensional families in the Stars. Why settle for a personality and a body as your identity, especially if they are wounded and dysfunctional? Become the observer; try to stay within universal law. Make your intent and focus Universal Peace, Brother/Sisterly Love, Equality, Freedom and Prosperity for All. Serve with gratitude the Creator in all Creation. Release the past, choose to awaken and heal. This will bring Heaven to Earth. Become the example then others will follow. Baba Ji once said the best contribution anyone can make to Earth is to live a thoroughly loving, joyous, abundant life. Nature is abundant. Do not settle for the ways of man.

Chapter 25
Ascension Myths

After 30 years of studying with Lamas, Yogis, Elders from many nations and almost every process oriented therapy I have come to the conclusion that many teachings have missing elements or dogmas that actually prevent ascension. Whole books have been written on the subject with extremes completely missing the point. Did you ever wonder why so many Yogis die? Have you ever seen a Priest, Pope, or Shaman ascend? How about a vegetarian, breatharian, a tree hugging goji berry eating, spandex wearing yuppie yogi? I am using a little humor to break people out of their boxes. When we look at the lives of the masters that actually did ascend we find they lived a life of balance. They were authentic and although some abstained, some indulged they all eventually came to terms with themselves and found balance. To some veggie Nazis I hate to burst your bubble but the Dali Lama eats meat. Many of them do, as well as have consorts. The Lamas have some of the most balanced teachings. The Native Americans also eat meat yet bless the animals, the food and make a sacrament out of it. There is a story about Buddha joining a sect that ate only grass and lived with the cows. One of the cows spoke to him and said, "What are you doing, you are not a cow, balance is the way." Personally my own preference is to eat less meat, closer to the ground and avoid processed foods especially non organic and GMOs a task nearly impossible in today's society. Especially when you are traveling. In severe cases of severe imbalance a strict raw vegetarian can often correct the imbalances. Many have cured life-threatening diseases using this method.

Everyone is different and we all have different needs depending on the necessities of the body, its genotype, etc. It is important to listen to the body, take care of the body. In today's world there are so many toxins, the water, food, the way it was prepared, even the air have become toxic therefore it is important to detoxify the body and do whatever is possible to avoid the toxins. In the days to come this will be reversed yet now we have to adjust to the world as it is.

If I have pissed anyone off yet I am doing my job because it is important to show ones judgments and limitations. Everything outside your beliefs, everything you have judged to be unholy or ungodly is God expressing itself. You can however choose to set boundaries with certain expressions of God. If a man/woman has chosen to be untruthful, imbalanced, or express in ways that are unfair, unjust, harmful to themselves or others you can choose to not participate. The trick is to do it in a way that is not defensive, condemning, judgmental or superior. It is called loving detachment. The wisdom we have gained through experience at times clearly reminds us this is a path we have already taken which creates a reality we do not want to or have already experienced. Many who come from the heart will feel automatically this is not the path for them. Your heart is where the soul resides and the soul is connected to source, your past lives, a vast amount of information and guidance if listened to will help you avoid many unpleasant situations. Many what some call negative events often were merely because one did not listen to the heart. It was only negative if you did not gain the wisdom from the experience.

In a dream I was told several keys to ascension. The first was to find balance. The second was to master judgment. The third was to transcend all cultural and religious boundaries, see the Creator in all creation, which attunes one to Unity Conscious. The last key was we have to not only see the divinity in others we have to own it within ourselves. This means every atom, molecule, cell, bone, tissue, including every organ in our personal body. We have to ground creator within every aspect of ourselves, love ourselves including the physical. So many in service mode forget to be kind to themselves, take care of their own needs. Again this is an imbalance.

The reason so many do not ascend is they forgot to take the body with them. They had a belief the body was not important, the illusion, withdrew their energy from it. When you do not feed something it dies and love is the food your body needs to ascend. They have to return through the birth canal in a process called reincarnation. This brings us back to mastering judgment, becoming the observer and allowing love to flow through a balanced body. This includes your physical body, mental body, emotional body, as well as your multidimensional spirit bodies. The higher dimensions are always pouring out love, joy, bliss and healing energies in service. Yet we have to ground it here. You do not ascend by judging things to be other than holy with the intention of rising above it. You ascend by grounding creator into every cell of your body, which creates a quickening. The body begins to vibrate faster and faster in this process. Eventually you become less dense physical, later evolve to an energy body, then a light body finally becoming pure consciousness. A simple explanation of the dimensions. Most important, be authentic. Do not worship external Gods, ascension is an internal process.

They will greet you along the way yet the ascension process stops when you shift to external. I love and respect the Masters, Saints and Sages. This includes the spiritually and technologically advanced off-worlders. Yet in this process I never forget the God within or give up my own personal God connection. This is the path to self- mastery and ascension. High five the masters.

Chapter 26
In Conclusion

We now have a golden opportunity to end the pain, suffering, poverty and enslavement on Earth. We have all we need. We have the wisdom, the healing and free energy technology, as well as the inspiration on high to truly create Heaven on Earth. There are billions of souls incarnate on Earth, who came from other advanced civilizations awakening, and transcending the matrix. There is a great plan, and it is as if God sent his best from the highest realms, to unify on Earth in this awakening and healing adventure.

We are going to have to set aside the wounded egos, the self-importance, the sense of entitlement, the false concept of separation. We are going to have to change our focus away from outer appearances, the manipulations and programming of the matrix. It is all about inner awareness, aligning with the soul and spirit being truly authentic and having the courage to live a life of impeccable integrity. We are going to have to realign ourselves individually and collectively with Universal Law, Universal Peace, Brotherly/Sisterly Love, Equality, Freedom and Prosperity for all. We are going to have to help those less fortunate if we are going to continue in this evolutionary process on Earth. It is imperative that each individual make their own personal God/ Spirit/ Creator connection and develop their own inner guidance and act on it. This is the only true security. The external security promised by the archons and the matrix is going to be the greatest insecurity in the days to come of those who depend upon it.

The days of tyranny are coming to a close. It is time to walk away and stop being a willing participant in anything that does not align with Universal Law. It is no longer an option if one wants to continue to participate or have any future on Earth. Hope this helps, please share with your family and friends. If you are interested further, I encourage you to order James's books through our website.www.eceti.org and for amazing videos of UFOs and other paranormal events go to the official ECETI StarGate You Tube site.

Also Check Out

ECETI Australia www.ecetiaustralia.org

JCETI www.jceti.org

More information can be found in the books Reunion with Source and Becoming Gods. www.eceti.org and www.lulu.com

About James Gilliland

James Gilliland is a best-selling author, internationally known lecturer, minister, counselor, multiple Near Death Experiencer and contactee. He is a facilitator of many Eastern disciplines; a visionary dedicated to the awakening and healing of Humanity and the Earth who teaches higher dimensional realities from experience. He was initiated by a venerable Lama, Guyaltrul Rinpoche and given the name Rigdzin Norbu, "Jewel of Pure Awareness."

James is recognized world-wide as the founder of the Gilliland Estate, previously referred to and commonly known as the ECETI Ranch (Enlightened Contact with ExtraTerrestrial Intelligence) where he documents and shares amazing multi-dimensional contact phenomenon which can be viewed at www.eceti.org. His weekly *As You Wish Talk Radio* program on BBSradio.com draws an audience from around the world interested in truth and Higher Consciousness.

James's books *Reunion with Source*, *Becoming Gods*, and *The Ultimate Soul Journey* educate, awaken, inform and heal. His latest book – *Anunnaki Return Star Nations and the Days to Come* is a powerful look at what is happening on a multi-dimensional level as we move forward in this time of great change.

He is the host of the documentary *Contact Has Begun* and has been featured in documentaries and television shows such as *His Story, The History Channel, UFOs then and Now, UFO Hotspots, ABC, Fox News, BBC Danny Dyer Special* and *Paranormal State.* He has also appeared on numerous radio shows including Coast to Coast and Jeff Rense. His unique focus on dispelling the myths propogated by the disinformation system make him an in-demand speaker at events such as the *International UFO Congress, Contact in the Desert* and the *Star Knowledge Conferences.*

An unprecedented event that has the potential to change the course and destiny of Humanity and the Earth is unfolding at the Gilliland Ranch near Mt Adams, and Trout Lake, Washington where UFO sightings, Orb phenomena, CE5 Contact and "UFO contact" with spiritually and technologically advanced extra and ultra-terrestrial off world visitors (a "greater family of man") has occurred and continues to occur on an ongoing basis. This message is shared annually at ECETI's popular **Science, Spirit and World Transformation Conference** hosted by James every summer at the Gilliland Estate.

The people of Earth are being offered a chance to join the rest of the universe in peace and participate in spiritual awakening and benevolent Extraterrestrial contact. James encourages you to be part of that change.

For other books by James, DVD's, conferences, updates and more go to www.eceti.org and www.privateinvitationeceti.com